BOOK ANALYSIS

Written by Tom O'Brien

As I Lay Dying

BY WILLIAM FAULKNER

Bright
≡Summaries.com

WILLIAM FAULKNER

- **Born in New Albany, Mississippi in 1897.**
- **Died in Byhalia, Mississippi in 1962.**
- **Notable works:**
  - *A Rose for Emily* (1930), short story
  - *The Sound and the Fury* (1929), novel
  - *Absalom, Absalom!* (1936), novel

Born William Cuthbert Falkner (the original spelling of his family name), the winner of the 1949 Nobel Prize in Literature grew up in a literary family while also learning to ride horses, hunt and fish. His strongest influences were his mother, who encouraged him to read and draw, and his nanny Caroline Barr.

He did not graduate from high school, and then managed to enlist in the Canadian Royal Airforce by pretending to be British, but World War I ended before he flew any active missions, which did not stop him from adopting the persona (and the uniform) of an RAF pilot when he returned to Mississippi.

Prior to 1926, when his debut novel *Soldiers' Pay* was published, he wrote mainly poetry and absorbed the work of modernists such as the British-American poet T. S. Elliot (1888-1965) and the Irish novelist James Joyce (1882-1941). He was advised by the writer Sherwood Anderson (1876-1941) to write stories based on the rural Mississippi country that included his home town of Oxford, advice which resulted in his creation of the fictional Yoknapatawpha County, which became the setting for the majority of his novels.

When he published the controversial novel *Sanctuary* in 1931, it sold well and aroused interest in his earlier novels such as *The Sound and the Fury* (1929). This book, and other novels published during the 1930s, such as *Light in August* (1932) and *Absalom, Absalom*! (1936), are usually considered Faulkner's best work, and have attracted more analyses and criticism than any other 20th century writer, due to his dense, challenging text full of symbolism, linguistic experimentation and deeply flawed characters.

Faulkner continued to write on difficult themes such as race, death and sexuality through the 1940s and 1950s. He died from thrombosis developed after a riding accident in 1962.

AS I LAY DYING

A TRAGICOMIC NOVEL

- **Genre:** Southern Gothic
- **Reference edition:** Faulkner, W. (1985) *As I Lay Dying: The Corrected Text*. New York: Vintage Books.
- **1st edition:** 1930
- **Themes:** life and death, family, words and language, community

Set in the same fictional Mississippi county as his previous two novels *Sartoris* (1929) and *The Sound and the Fury* (1929), William Faulkner's fifth novel *As I Lay Dying* shifts the focus away from the county's most prominent aristocratic families to the poor, uneducated farmers struggling to make a living from their small patches of land.

Anse Bundren, his grownup children and young son Vardaman travel from their backwoods farm to Yoknapatawpha County's largest town in order to fulfil the dying wish of Anse's wife

Addie to be buried alongside her blood relatives. Incompetent, lazy, and far from sincere in his commitment to his wife's dying wishes, Anse puts his sons and daughter in danger and relies heavily on the charitable goodwill of neighbours and strangers alike, who are increasingly horrified as Addie's body starts to decompose. Once in Jefferson, Anse reveals an ulterior motive in coming to town, and loses one of his sons to the insane asylum.

15 different narrators chart the Bundrens' trip across the county, offering unique perspectives from both within and outside the Bundren family. In particular, Faulkner uses the deeper reflections and powerful perception of Anse and Addie's second-oldest son Darl to add depth and complexity to the darkly comic farce of the novel's events.

SUMMARY

THE DEATH OF ADDIE BUNDREN

Addie Bundren is close to death as she watches her oldest son Cash build her own coffin from the window of the family home on the side of a small mountain in rural Mississippi. She is watched over by her daughter Dewey Dell, who is concealing her pregnancy, and Cora Tull, a neighbour who disapproves of Addie and most of her family due to their lack of (in her view) religious piety. Vernon Tull, Cora's husband, and Addie's toothless husband Anse, who has so far refused to bring a doctor to help his dying wife, sit on the porch. Darl and Jewel, two more of Addie's sons, prepare to take a load of timber to sell, despite their mother's impending death. Darl watches Jewel prepare his horse, which remains half wild and cannot be controlled by anyone else. Addie's youngest son Vardaman returns from a fishing trip with his catch.

After Darl and Jewel leave, Addie's health deteriorates and Anse is finally forced to bring in the doctor. The obese Dr Peabody immediately realises that Addie will not live much longer, and the Bundrens gather by the bed as she takes her last breath. Miles away, Darl seems to sense his mother's death (just as he sensed his sister's pregnancy without being told) and tells Jewel as they struggle through a torrential rainstorm with their wagon. None of Anse, Cash or Dewey Dell seem to react strongly to Addie's death; Anse orders Cash to complete the coffin and Dewey Dell to make dinner.

Vardaman is horrified, refusing to accept that his mother is really dead. In his hysteria, he lets Dr Peabody's mules loose with his wagon, and begins to confuse his mother with the enormous fish that he caught and killed earlier that day. At their farm a few miles away down the mountain's slope, Vernon and Cora Tull's night is disturbed first by Dr Peabody's mules and empty wagon, and then by the arrival of Vardaman at their door. They bring him home as the weather worsens, and Vernon Tull helps Cash to complete the coffin in the pouring rain as the helpless Anse watches on. In the morning, they discover that Vardaman has drilled air holes in the coffin's lid.

Anse announces his intention to fulfil Addie's dying wish of being buried in Jefferson, 40 miles away, with her relatives. After Cash repairs the coffin, there is a small funeral at which the Bundrens' male neighbours discuss Anse's general uselessness, and the women sing hymns.

THE JOURNEY TO JEFFERSON, STAGE ONE: WATER

When Darl and Jewel return, the family sets off in their wagon with Addie's coffin. Jewel refuses to ride with the rest of the family, instead following the wagon on his horse. As the bridge across the river near their home has been washed away in the storm, they are forced to travel miles out of their way to the next bridge, which they discover has also been washed away. Samson, at whose farm they stay the night, is the first to notice that Addie's corpse is beginning to smell. Returning to the river near Vernon Tull's farm, Anse, Vardaman, Dewey Dell and Vernon cross the river on the remains of the bridge, while Cash, Darl and Jewel take the wagon further downstream where the river is shallower.

As the three brothers work out how to get the wagon across the river, Darl reminisces about how Jewel acquired his horse. When Jewel was 15 years old, he began to fall asleep regularly during his days' work, and his mother and siblings were forced to take over most of his tasks. Cash and Darl initially suspected that Jewel was involved with a local woman, but really he was working at night in the fields of the Snopes family, the wealthiest farmers in the region, in order to make enough money to buy one of the Snopes' famous Texan horses. Even though he neglected his work on his own family's farm, Jewel believes that he owns the horse outright, and refuses to let anyone else take any of the responsibility for feeding and looking after it.

The three brothers attempt to take the wagon across the river, with Jewel picking out the safest route on his horse, but the current is too strong and begins to turn the wagon over. The mules are drowned, and only Cash is able to stay with the wagon, desperately trying to prevent his mother's coffin being washed away. With Vernon's help, Darl and Jewel are able to recover both Cash and the coffin from the water, but their mules are gone and Cash's leg is badly broken. Jewel rides to Armstid's, the nearest farm, and returns with another team of mules. With Cash laid on top of the coffin in the badly damaged wagon, the family ride to Armstid's farm.

THE JOURNEY TO JEFFERSON, STAGE TWO: FIRE

With the wagon stored in Armstid's barn, and Addie's corpse now decaying rapidly, Anse travels to meet with Snopes to negotiate for a new team of mules. While he is gone, Vardaman becomes obsessed with the buzzards that are drawn to his mother's body, and Jewel, unable to locate Dr Peabody, instead fetches a horse doctor who performs rudimentary, and extremely painful, surgery on Cash's broken leg. When Anse returns, he claims to have bought a team of mules from Snopes. Pressed by Armstid to reveal how he paid for the team, he reveals that the return of Jewel's horse to Snopes was a part of the bargain. Jewel is furious, but eventually leaves the horse in Snopes' barn himself.

The Bundrens are forced to take another detour through the town of Mottson due to the flood. Here, Dewey Dell visits a drugstore where she attempts to convince the pharmacist to give her something to terminate her pregnancy, which he refuses to do. Her older brothers buy some cement to try and improvise a cast and stop the flow of blood from Cash's wounded leg. The town's residents are disgusted by the now un- bearable smell of Addie's body and the state of Cash's leg, and the family are forced to move on.

The Bundrens stop at the Gillespies', another family farm, where Vardaman appears to share with Darl the experience of hearing their mother praying from inside her coffin, and Darl taunts Jewel with his knowledge (apparently gained through intui- tion) that he was fathered by someone other than Anse. That night, the Gillespies' barn is set alight. Jewel takes the lead in rescuing all the animals from the resulting fire before finally removing his mother's coffin from the flames, badly burning his back in the process. The knowledge that Darl started the fire spreads from Vardaman, who saw him do it, to the rest of the family as they finally approach the town of Jefferson.

THE END OF THE JOURNEY

In Jefferson, Addie is finally buried alongside her relatives, after Anse borrows two spades from a house where music is playing. Outside the cemetery, men are waiting to arrest Darl for setting fire to the Gillespies' barn. When he resists, Dewey Dell, to Cash's surprise, attacks Darl and helps the men subdue him. Darl is taken away, laughing hysterically, bound for the insane asylum in Jackson, and Cash suspects that it was Dewey Dell who informed the authorities of Darl's role in the fire.

Dewey Dell visits another drugstore, and this time a pharmacist's assistant agrees to give her an abortion. However, when she returns after closing time, the assistant demands sex in return for his help, and Dewey Dell realises that she has been tricked. When she returns to her family, Anse sees the money the father of her child had given her for the abortion and takes it for himself.

Anse returns the spades and tells his sons and daughter to prepare to leave town, before going off on a mysterious errand. Later, he returns to the wagon and Cash realises realise that Anse has spent the money he took from Dewey Dell on a shave, a haircut and a set of new false teeth. He is accompanied by the woman from the house where the music was playing, whom he introduces to them as their new stepmother.

CHARACTER STUDY

A note on this character study:

The character of Darl Bundren narrates 19 of the novel's 59 chapters, and is strikingly different to the other narrators in that he apparently has access to the secret knowledge of other members of the Bundren family, and is able to narrate scenes at which he is not physically present. Because the character of Darl is so intimately related Faulkner's narrative structure and techniques, a more complete analysis of his character can be found in the analysis section of this guide; the brief character study in this section just deals with his actions within the story and the other characters' relationships to him.

ADDIE BUNDREN

Addie is a former school teacher, wife to Anse and mother to Cash, Darl, Jewel, Dewey Dell and Vardaman. Although she is dying as the story opens, and features only as a decaying corpse in most of the rest of the novel, she is nevertheless a central character; she provides the motivation for the family to make the trip to Jefferson, and we learn more about her character through the memories of her son Darl and neighbour Cora Tull, and the single section of the novel that she narrates posthumously.

In her life as a school teacher before marrying Anse, Addie was mostly unhappy, living under the influence of her father's attitude to life, which was "that the reason for living was to get ready to stay dead for a long time" (p. 155). The only way she feels she can make a mark on people's lives is when she physically punishes the students in her care, taking a kind of sadistic 'pleasure' from these acts. She brutally summarises her marriage to Anse with the four words "So I took Anse" (p. 156), indicating that she never loved him. This is confirmed when she describes how she felt that her children with Anse were a violation of her "aloneness" (p. 158), but that her child (Jewel) with another man gave her a sense of comfort and love that she could not feel with her and Anse's children. The special attachment she feels to Jewel is reciprocated: in Jewel's only narration, he describes a powerful wish that he and she were alone in the world without the rest of the family.

In Cora Tull's eyes, Addie is not enough of a committed Christian, and lacks the humility required (in Cora's view) to be a good wife and mother. Darl, likewise, chooses to relate a memory where she fails to conceal her preference toward Jewel, showing his mother in a negative light. Vernon Tull and Dr Peabody have a much more sympathetic view of Addie, believing that her years living with Anse wore her down until she was quite ready to die to escape him.

ANSE BUNDREN

Anse Bundren is an ineffectual man, a lazy and unskilled farmer who relies heavily on his family and neighbours while at the same time believing strongly in his own parental authority and independence. To Addie's younger self he appears "like a tall bird hunched in the cold weather" (p. 156) due to his hunchbacked spine, and his son Darl adds to the impression of physical deformity by describing his father's feet as "badly splayed, his toes cramped and bent and warped, with no toenails at all on his little toes" (p. 10).

Anse's view of his own character is utterly at odds with the perspective of his neighbours and the people who help the Bundrens on their trip to Jefferson. Anse reflects that "I always is fed me and mine and kept a roof above us" (p. 32), whereas his neighbours feel that God and, by extension, themselves, have looked after Anse and his family for so long that it has become a habit. Likewise, Anse remarks on the botched treatment of Cash's broken leg, saying "I just aimed to help him" (p. 206), but later Dr Peabody says to Cash: "Why didn't Anse carry you to the sawmill and stick your leg in the saw? [...] then you could have stuck his head in the saw and cured a whole family" (p. 223).

The sense of Anse's selfishness is compounded by his resentment of his three older sons for showing signs of independence: Cash for becoming a skilled carpenter, Darl for trying make his own way, and Jewel for working independently to buy his horse. He also cruelly manipulates Dewey Dell into giving him the money intended for her abortion, using it to satisfy his own desires.

Like Jason Compson in *The Sound and the Fury*, Faulkner uses the contrast of Anse's self-righteousness with his ridiculousness in the eyes of his family and neighbours to darkly comic effect.

CASH

Cash is the eldest son of Addie and Anse. He is a skilled carpenter and has a strongly practical side that is only matched in the family by Jewel's ability with horses. His practicality is taken to an almost absurd extreme when he describes in intricate detail the carpentry of his mother's coffin. That this is a vital part of his identity is confirmed when he is terrified that his tools have been lost when the Bundrens attempt to cross the flooded river.

In stark contrast to his father, Cash has a great appetite for work and is willing to sacrifice a great deal for the good of his family, also proving highly resistant to pain and physical discomfort when he is badly injured on the way to Jefferson. Cash's physical suffering, his identity as a carpenter, and his tolerance for the shortcomings of his family members lend his character an almost Christ-like quality; even though he is horrified by Darl's burning of the Gillespies' barn, he manages to find some sympathy for his brother, and is critical of Anse, Jewel and Dewey Dell's violent rejection of Darl. This is further reinforced by the absence of any ulterior motive in Cash's dedication to the cause of bringing his mother's body to Jefferson, which he shares only with Jewel.

DARL

Darl is Cash's younger brother by approximately two years. He seems to be the only Bundren apart from his mother Addie who is capable of deep thought, but unlike Addie, who reflects on her own life and personality, he tends to make observations on the world around him, including an almost obsessive focus on the actions of his brother Jewel; Darl begins many of his chapters with 'he', meaning Jewel, or by addressing Jewel directly.

At the beginning of the novel, Darl has a pre-existing reputation for strangeness, which is recognised by Vernon Tull, but rejected by Cora Tull, who believes that Darl is the only Bundren with any redeeming qualities. Vernon Tull's observation seems to be the more reliable, since Cora's belief that it was Anse who insisted on Jewel and Darl's trip to sell wood is false, and it was actually Darl who insisted that they go, apparently wishing for Jewel to miss the moment of his mother's death out of spite.

Darl initially works hard and in harmony with his brothers Cash and Jewel to overcome the problems of the journey to Jefferson, but does not share their full commitment to the goal of getting their mother's body to its final resting place. In the river, he abandons the wagon, leaving Cash to protect the coffin and Jewel to rescue it when the cart is finally overturned completely. At the Gillespies' farm he seems to succumb to madness, half-heartedly assisting Jewel in his heroic rescue of Addie's coffin and the Gillespies' animals from the fire which he himself started, seemingly in order to sabotage the final stages of the journey.

After the incident at the Gillespies' farm, both Jewel and Dewey Dell's suspicions about Darl are confirmed, and they get their revenge for his taunting of Dewey Dell over her pregnancy, and Jewel over his paternity, by assisting the police in Darl's arrest. Cash is more philosophical about his brother's madness, while Anse clearly sees a mentally unstable son as a threat to his desire for a more comfortable life.

JEWEL

Jewel is Addie's middle child, approximately ten years younger than Darl, but is not Anse's son, a fact known only to Addie, the Reverend Whitfield (Jewel's biological father) and to Darl (through his special ability to sense uncomfortable truths). The novel opens with Darl describing how much taller Jewel is compared with himself, emphasising this with a comic description of Jewel stepping directly through the windows of a building instead of taking the path around it, which immediately sets Jewel apart from his brother, both in his physical size and refusal to take the easy, conventional course.

Due to Darl's preoccupation with his brother's character and actions, arising from his jealousy over Jewel's position as his mother's favourite and intuitive doubts about his paternity, Jewel is physically described in far more detail than any other character. Darl often uses wood to describe Jewel's appearance: "his pale eyes like wood set into his wooden face" (p. 1), and "He sits erect on the seat, leaning a little forward, wooden-backed" (p. 84). This woodenness represents both Jewel's hard, impenetrable character, and his role as the chief protector of his mother after her death, along with the wooden coffin, so well-made by Cash that it survives the disasters of the journey to Jefferson.

Jewel spends most of the novel in a barely-supressed rage, and is the only character to consistently swear, punctuating his speech with 'goddamn' and 'son of a bitch'. His constant anger reflects Addie's rage at having sacrificed, due to loneliness, her middle-class schoolteacher's life to marry the bumbling Anse. Not being a Bundren by blood, Jewel cannot develop his own version of Darl's philosophical attitude towards the family's undignified poverty-stricken lifestyle, neither can he match Cash's tolerance, nor share in Anse, Dewey Dell and Vardaman's ignorance of the possibility of any other way of living. He strives so hard to get his mother's body to Jefferson because he, consciously or unconsciously, shares the desire for revenge against Anse that inspired Addie's insistence on her burial there.

DEWEY DELL

Dewey Dell is Cash, Darl and Jewel's younger sister, who is in her late teens. As the book opens, she is performing the menial task of keeping her dying mother cool with a fan, but is far more concerned with how to solve the problem of her unwanted pregnancy than by her mother's impending death.

In one sense, Dewey Dell elicits the same kind of sympathy as Caddy Compson in *The Sound and the Fury*, Faulkner's favourite among all the characters he created. Dewey Dell, like Caddy, is an attractive young woman – remarked upon by both Mosely and Magowan, workers in the two drugstores where she attempts to get an abortion – whose sexuality ("I felt like a wet seed wild in the hot blind earth", p. 58) is at odds with her family's and her society's attitude towards female sexuality.

In another sense, however, Dewey Dell exhibits the same kind of ignorance and selfishness as her father. The illogical reasoning in her justification for succumbing to her sexual desire with Lafe, the father of her unborn child, reflects her father's muddled idea that the road to their house is the cause of his (in reality, self-inflicted) problems. Her desire to find a solution that would allow her life to go on just as before is mirrored in Anse's constant seeking out of the least taxing solutions to his problems. It is interesting to consider whether the contrast between the path of 'noble suffering' chosen by the aristocratic Caddy Compson in *The Sound and the Fury*, and the path of least resistance chosen by the lower-class, 'white trash' Dewey Dell Bundren in *As I Lay Dying*, is illustrative of Faulkner's own prejudice, or whether the author is sympathetic to Dewey Dell's restricted options in the much harsher environment in which she lives her life.

VARDAMAN

Vardaman is Addie and Anse's youngest son, whose age is difficult to determine but is most likely not yet ten years old. He is the only one of the Bundrens who exhibits a 'natural' reaction to his mother's death, including horror, denial and rage. He does not receive any comfort from his family immediately after the death, when Cash goes straight on with the construction of the coffin, Dewey Dell is wrapped up in her own concerns, and Anse seems to have forgotten Vardaman entirely.

Vardaman is therefore left to form his own ideas about his mother's death, his childish reasoning leading him to the contradictory conclusions, first that Dr Peabody killed his mother, second that she is not really dead, and third, mixed up in his mind with the fish he recently caught and killed, that "my mother is a fish" (p. 74). He instinctively knows that something is wrong with his family's reaction to the death, and runs through the rainstorm to the Tulls' home, where he finally gets some of the compassion that he needs.

Later in the novel, the sections narrated by Vardaman offer a child's perspective on the fire at the Gillespies', Dewey Dell's unsuccessful efforts to secure an abortion, and Darl's arrest. In these scenes, Vardaman is unaware of most of the key details, but – perhaps because of this – makes small observations missed by the adult characters, further enriching these scenes. His character's perspective is a kind of midpoint between Benjy Compson's complete lack of adult comprehension in *The Sound and the Fury*, and the kind of deep reflections shared by Vardaman's older brother Darl, and Benjy's brother Quentin Compson.

CORA TULL

Cora Tull is the Bundrens' pious Christian neighbour and Vernon Tull's wife. In the first chapter that she narrates, she describes in detail the baking of some cakes to sell, displaying the same obsessive attention to detail as Cash Bundren does towards his carpentry. Her character functions as an unreliable narrator, and her frequent mis-observations, sometimes comical, serve as a caricature of an interfering busybody who makes definitive judgments based on incomplete information. The most amusing of these (as soon as we learn the truth in the next chapter) is when she mistakes the Reverend Whitfield's affair with Addie for him "[wrestling] with her [Addie's] spirit" and "[striving] with the vanity in her mortal heart" (p. 152).

She also displays a certain hypocrisy, such as when she recalls chiding Addie Bundren for her lack of a proper Christian attitude. Within the space of one short dialogue she says to Addie that her "conduct is not pleasing to [God]" (p. 152), but then asks rhetorically "Who are you to say what is sin and what is not sin?" (*ibid.*), not realising she is demanding from Addie the same kind of humility which she herself lacks.

Despite her judgmental attitude, Cora displays toward Vardaman the basic humanity that he needs but does not receive from his family.

VERNON TULL

Vernon Tull is the Bundrens' neighbour and Cora's husband. He shares his wife's disapproval of Anse Bundren, but does not judge in the same strict, religious way that his wife does, which makes him more reliable as a narrator. Because of his objectivity and the sympathy he shows towards Addie and Vardaman, the strangeness of the rest of the Bundrens through his eyes takes on added weight. Like other neighbours, Vernon has a long history of helping Anse Bundren when he (inevitably) needs it, and sometimes employs Anse's sons for jobs on his own, more successful farm.

The owners of three more farms where the Bundrens stay on their way to Jefferson (Samson, Armstid and Gillespie) have essentially the same character traits as Vernon Tull: they are decent men who would never refuse to help a person, but at the same time are shocked by the Bundrens' odd behaviour.

DR PEABODY

Dr Peabody is a recurring character in Faulkner's fictional Yoknapatawpha County. He is massively overweight, and lives in more or less the same basic poverty as his clients because of their inability to pay him much for his services. Of all the characters that know the Bundrens well, he is the most openly critical of Anse's behaviour, particularly of Anse's refusal to call for him until it is too late to save Addie, and his refusal to get proper treatment for Cash's broken leg.

ANALYSIS

NARRATIVE TECHNIQUE

As I Lay Dying is narrated by 15 different characters in 59 chapters. The narration of 39 of these chapters is (unevenly) divided between Anse, Cash, Jewel, Dewey Dell and Vardaman Bundren on the one hand, and a variety of characters from outside the family on the other. The Bundrens' chapters are mostly written in the present tense, and use a stream-of-consciousness technique, where the writer attempts to represent the inner thoughts of a character as well as their descriptions of events. The chapters narrated by outside characters are written mostly in the past tense, and tend to focus on the Bundrens rather than those characters' own concerns, but still represent the thoughts and feelings of those characters in a fairly uncomplicated manner. These two types of narrative complement each other, with the reader experiencing a more intimate relationship with the Bundrens (whether they want to or not!), and then gaining a wider perspective (and more concrete information) on the Bundrens and their journey from the other characters. Faulkner seems to have ordered and blended these perspectives to maintain a certain level of narrative tension and suspense (of not knowing) while also allowing the reader to follow the narrative relatively comfortably, only really challenged by Vardaman's childish perspective and racing thoughts.

However, Faulkner complicates his use of narrative technique in the 19 chapters narrated by Darl. In Darl's case, though he is a Bundren, some of the immediacy of the other Bundrens' narratives, their 'in-the-moment' thoughts and feelings, is missing, replaced by more thoughtful and detailed descriptions of his surroundings, and his focus on his brother Jewel rather than himself. Even more striking is Darl's ability to give a detailed account of scenes at which he is not physically present, such as the moment of his mother's death, and to access the secret knowledge of his family members. José Angel García Landa has written that "Darl's reportorial speech, his omniscience, the frequency and even distribution of his voice, all make him a surrogate authorial narrator, with a problematical existence in this world of perspective" (Garcia, 1990: 66). There are several plausible answers to the question 'Why would Faulkner insert a character with a 'problematical existence' into a story whose narrative structure (or 'world of perspective') otherwise functions quite seamlessly?', but three possibilities are:

1. **Because he felt like it!** Faulkner, who wrote *As I Lay Dying* late at night over a six-week period, perhaps simply needed a 'surrogate authorial narrator' to complement the perspectives of the simple country folk who make up the protagonists of the story. Which of the other Bundrens or their neighbours could realistically provide the reader with such vivid, poetic descriptions of the flooded river or the burning barn, and give these events the centrality to the story that they deserve? And would Addie's death scene have satisfied the writer (or the reader) had it been described from the perspective of Anse? It could be argued that Darl's unrealistic descriptive abilities were artistically necessary to Faulkner.

2. **To challenge the living Bundrens.** Everyone outside the Bundren family (with the exception of the pharmacist's assistant, who uses trickery to seduce Dewey Dell) is horrified by their behaviour, but being 'good Christians' (or a good doctor in Peabody's case), are unable to refuse to help them. The character of Darl, who threatens Jewel and Dewey Dell with impossible knowledge of their secrets and attempts to sabotage the journey to Jefferson, perhaps represents a balancing force against the awfulness of Anse and the meekness of those who allow him to get away with his actions. The tragedy of the novel's resolution is that Anse is ultimately victorious, and Darl's character is 'kicked out' of the narrative so that Anse can bring it to a resolution that satisfies his needs, with the assistance of Jewel and Dewey Dell, who are also threatened by Darl's 'problematic existence'.

3. **To challenge Addie Bundren.** Addie's wish to be buried with her relatives is the motivating factor behind the trip to Jefferson (even if it is merely an excuse for some of the Bundrens to visit the town), which she reveals in her chapter to be her revenge on Anse for the

uncomfortable and unfulfilling life that she had with him. The character of Darl challenges Addie's control over the narrative—symbolised by her rotting corpse—by subtle (at the river) and overt (at the Gillespies' farm) attempts to get rid of her presence. With this conflict, Faulkner adds a layer of high drama to the low farce of carrying a dead body through rural Mississippi, using Darl's 'unrealism' to do so.

LIFE AND DEATH

If the chapters narrated by Darl add a *technical* complexity to Faulkner's writing in *As I Lay Dying* that is worthy of analysis, the single chapter narrated by Addie Bundren adds a *thematic* complexity that is also worth looking at. The nature of life and death is one of the two major and closely related themes running through Addie's chapter (the other being the emptiness of words: see the analysis below), and Faulkner's positioning of Addie's chapter at the approximate midpoint of the novel means that other character's attitudes towards life and death should be analysed in relation to Addie's.

Theresa M. Towner writes of *As I Lay Dying* that "the book's title and Addie's chapter imply that dying and living are the same hopeless, pointless, doomed processes" (Towner, 2008: 27). The source of this attitude in Addie seems to be her father, who believes that "the reason for living is to get ready to stay dead for a long time" (p. 155), implying a lack of belief in any kind of meaningful afterlife. This would seem to explain Addie's conflicted relationship with Cora Tull, who would perhaps reply to Addie's father that the reason for living is to get ready to live in heaven forever. The way that Addie lives her life suggests her hopelessness, her sense of doom, but does not, however, suggest that she believes her life is entirely pointless. Even though she sees Cash's birth as a violation, she also believes that it made her whole, a feeling that she regained with even greater intensity in her affair with the reverend Whitfield and the birth of Jewel. When she says of Anse that "then he died. He did not know he was dead" (p. 160), she is implying that Anse – and perhaps, by extension, Darl, Dewey Dell and Vardaman – is not taking part in the experience of living a painful but ultimately meaningful life that she shares with Jewel (and perhaps Cash); Anse and the children that she feels no attachment to have lives that are hopeless, doomed and pointless.

When Addie dies, the reactions of Anse, Cash and Dewey Dell seem to confirm Addie's attitude to life and death in the periods when she felt she was not living (outside of Cash's infancy and her relationships with Whitfield and Jewel). Their lack of grief and immediate attention to mundane tasks implies that they never really 'lived' with Addie and that her death therefore causes them no real pain.

In contrast, even though the single chapter narrated by Jewel occurs before Addie's death, we can see in his attitude to life that he has inherited through his mother's blood a similar attitude to hers, rather than succumbing to the 'non-life' of the Bundrens in general. Jewel imagines him and his dying mother away from the others and says "it would just be me and her on a high hill and me rolling the rocks down the hill at the faces" (p. 14). Jewel's relationship with his horse, and the sacrifices that he made to buy it, are the strongest example in the novel of Addie's conception of what it really is to live.

Because of his perceptiveness, Darl is able to sense the 'true living' that Jewel shares with his mother and his horse, but we can see that he feels that he cannot share in this when he says "I don't know what I am. I don't know if I am or not. Jewel knows he is" (p. 72). Darl can neither share the dumb ignorance of Anse and Dewey Dell, nor the real emotional experiences of Jewel. This tension is perhaps the source of both his vindictiveness towards Jewel and Dewey Dell and his later insanity.

If most of the Bundrens' strange attitudes towards life and death can be assessed in terms of Addie's ideas in her central chapter, Vardaman's reaction to his mother's death is far more 'natural' and not subject to the internal logic of the narrative. His 'acting out'—blaming the doctor, vandalising his wagon, and drilling air holes in his mother's coffin—is recognizable to anyone who knows a child who has lost a parent at a young age, and his disordered associations that lead him to the idea that "my mother is a fish" (p. 74) read like a genuine attempt by Faulkner to follow a childlike train of thought to its conclusion. Chapters such as Vardaman's, in which concerns about character and narrative coherency are put aside in an attempt to record truths about human thoughts and experiences, are part of the reason why Faulkner's best works are still so celebrated throughout the English-speaking world, despite their focus on dysfunctional families in a tiny section of rural Mississippi.

EMPTY WORDS

The other main theme that can be explored both backward and forward in the novel from the base of Addie's chapter is her ideas about the emptiness of words. When Cash was born, Addie says:

> "That was when I learned that words are no good; that they don't fit even what they are trying to say at. When he was born, I knew that motherhood was invented by someone who had to have a word for it because the ones who had the children didn't care whether they had a word for it or not. I knew that fear was invented by someone who had never had the fear; pride, who had never had the pride." (pp. 157-158)

Just as with her ideas about life and death, the centrality of Addie's narration, and its startling difference from any other chapter, invite us to assess the other characters in the novel, her husband Anse in particular, in terms of her philosophy of language; are they an example of 'someone who had to have a word for it', or are they the one of those 'who didn't care whether they had a word for it or not'?

Anse Bundren is an extreme example of someone who uses words when he has never truly experienced what those words signify. Apart from Addie's direct accusations in her chapter, we can find many examples of the emptiness of Anse's words in the rest of the novel. When he uses words associated with work, money, exchange and value, he betrays either his lack of understanding of the concepts those words are supposed to signify, or a deliberate, cynical misuse of those words to justify his selfishness:

- Anse remembers Cash having an accident and not being able to work, and recalls "me and Addie <u>slaving and a-slaving</u>" (p. 32; emphasis added). From the events of the novel, and from every other character's observations, we know that Anse has no idea what it is to 'slave'; even in his own thoughts, Anse's words are empty of meaning.

- Anse says to Samson, when he tries to persuade the Bundrens to sleep in his house "we wouldn't be <u>beholden</u> [...] I thank you kindly" (p. 103; emphasis added). Anse is using the word 'beholden' in such a way as to imply that he does not want to owe Samson anything for his hospitality, but his behaviour throughout the novel betrays the fact that he has no understanding of the value of the help he receives from his neighbours, or what it means to owe anyone anything.
- To the Bundrens' next host on their journey, Armstid, Anse says "I know it's an <u>imposition</u> on you" (p. 168; emphasis added). Anse tries to demonstrate his awareness of the trouble that Armstid is going to in accommodating the Bundrens, but the reader (and probably Armstid) is fully aware of the emptiness of his words.

In contrast to Anse, Jewel is the primary example of someone who understands concepts through lived experience of them. The work he does late at night to pay for his horse is a real example of 'slaving', and his refusal to accept any help from his family or anyone else in feeding or looking after the horse arises from a genuine desire not to be 'beholden'. Jewel's horse is a living embodiment of value, and Anse demonstrates his complete ignorance of the true concept of value when he bargains away the horse without a second thought.

In her chapter, Addie also applies her theory of words to people's names:

> "And when I would think Cash and Darl that way until their names would die and solidify into a shape and then fade away. I would say, All right. It doesn't matter. It doesn't matter what they call them." (p. 159)

Given Addie's insistence that names do not matter, it is perhaps significant that Darl uses her full name when he taunts Jewel with "do you know that Addie Bundren is going to die?" (p. 36), and "Jewel, Addie Bundren is dead" (p. 48). Darl is perhaps using her full name because he never experienced with Addie the 'wordlessness' of an intimate mother/son relationship. This is in contrast to Jewel, who does not even use the words 'ma' or 'mother' in his single chapter (pp. 13-14), because he, unlike Darl, "[does] not care whether [he] has a word for it or not" (p. 157).

FURTHER REFLECTION

SOME QUESTIONS TO THINK ABOUT...

- Some critics have proposed the idea that the Bundrens' journey to Jefferson can be read entirely as a figment of Addie's imagination 'as she lies dying'. What do you think of this idea?
- When Faulkner has Darl talk about himself in the third person (pp. 235-236), is it simply the writer's intention to portray Darl's insanity? Are there other possible interpretations?
- What is Faulkner's intention in having the other farmers be, without exception, so helpful and accommodating to the Bundrens?
- In Vardaman's chapters, how successful is Faulkner in trying to represent the thought processes of a child?
- At the end of the novel, the Bundrens, apart from Darl, appear ready to return home. If the narrative were to continue, do you think that Jewel would return home with his family? Why? Why not?

- In the novel's final page, Cash says of Darl that "this world is not his world; this life his life" (p. 242). What do think Cash (or Faulkner) means by this?
- Look up and read the short poem 'This Be the Verse' by Phillip Larkin (British poet, 1922-1985). How much of the blame for the Bundren siblings' faults lies with their father, and how much with their mother?

We want to hear from you!
Leave a comment on your online library
and share your favourite books on social media!

FURTHER READING

REFERENCE EDITION

- Faulkner, W. (1930) *As I Lay Dying: The Corrected Text*. New York: Vintage Books.

REFERENCE STUDIES

- García Landa, J. A. (1990) Reflexivity in the narrative technique of *As I Lay Dying*. *English Language Notes*, 27(4).

- Towner, T. (2008). *The Cambridge Introduction to William Faulkner*. Cambridge: Cambridge University Press. [Online]. [Accessed 15 November 2018]. Available from: <https://doi.org/10.1017/CBO9780511817045>

ADDITIONAL SOURCES

- Cohn, D. (1979) *Transparent Minds: Narrative Modes for Presenting Consciousness in Fiction*. New Jersey: Princeton University Press.

- Lewis, P. (2007). *The Cambridge Introduction to Modernism*. Cambridge: Cambridge University Press.

ADAPTATIONS

- *As I Lay Dying.* (2013) [Film]. James Franco. Dir. USA: RabbitBandini Productions. Picture Entertainment.

MORE FROM BRIGHTSUMMARIES.COM

- Reading guide – *The Sound and the Fury* by William Faulkner.

www.brightsummaries.com

Ebook EAN: 9782808016056

Paperback EAN: 9782808016063

Legal Deposit: D/2018/12603/563

Cover: © Primento

Digital conception by Primento, the digital partner of publishers.